BEHIND THE BRAND

FENDER

Fender PLAY™

Choose your instrument.
Pick a style.
Get started on your path.

WHAT WILL YOU PLAY?

ACOUSTIC

BY SARA GREEN

BELLWETHER MEDIA • MINNEAPOLIS, MN

Blastoff! Discovery launches a new mission: reading to learn. Filled with facts and features, each book offers you an exciting new world to explore!

BLASTOFF! UNIVERSE

BLASTOFF! Beginners — GRADE K

BLASTOFF! READERS — GRADES 1-3

BLASTOFF! DISCOVERY — GRADE 4

This edition first published in 2024 by Bellwether Media, Inc.

No part of this publication may be reproduced in whole or in part without written permission of the publisher.
For information regarding permission, write to Bellwether Media, Inc., Attention: Permissions Department,
6012 Blue Circle Drive, Minnetonka, MN 55343.

Library of Congress Cataloging-in-Publication Data

Names: Green, Sara, 1964- author.
Title: Fender / Sara Green.
Description: Minneapolis : Bellwether Media, 2024. | Series: Behind the brand | Includes bibliographical references and index. |
  Audience: Ages 7-13 | Audience: Grades 4-6 | Summary: "Engaging images accompany information about Fender. The combination of high interest subject matter and narrative text is intended for students in grades 3 through 8"–Provided by publisher.
Identifiers: LCCN 2023045233 (print) | LCCN 2023045234 (ebook)
  | ISBN 9798886878080 (library binding) | ISBN 9798886879544 (paperback) | ISBN 9798886879025 (ebook)
Subjects: LCSH: Fender Musical Instruments–History–Juvenile literature.
Classification: LCC ML404.F46 G74 2024 (print) | LCC ML404.F46 (ebook) | DDC 787.87/1973–dc23/20230925
LC record available at https://lccn.loc.gov/2023045233
LC ebook record available at https://lccn.loc.gov/2023045234

Editor: Betsy Rathburn   Designer: Andrea Schneider

Printed in the United States of America, North Mankato, MN.

TABLE OF CONTENTS

ROCKING IT!

Four friends are ready to play their first concert. They have created a band to perform a song. After weeks of practice, they are ready to play it in front of an audience. They cannot wait to get on stage!

The lights dim as the band takes the stage. The crowd begins to buzz as the band plays together. Their song features a guitar solo. The lead guitarist plays it on their Fender electric guitar. Their fingers fly across the **fretboard** during the solo. The crowd goes wild!

– – FRETBOARD

THE BIRTH OF FENDER

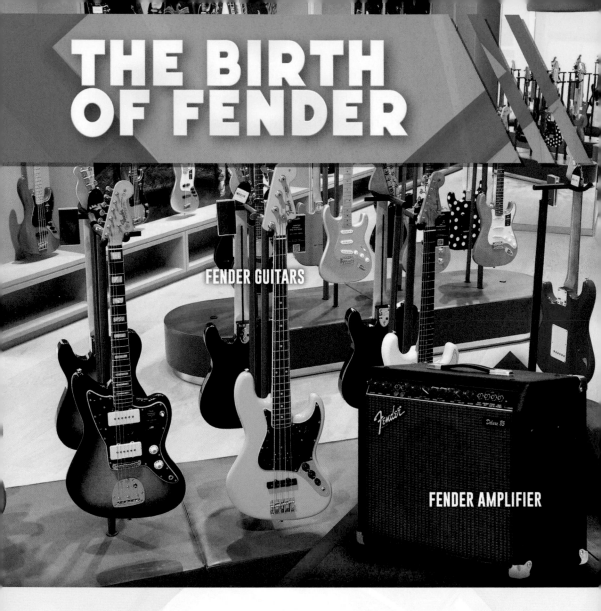

FENDER GUITARS

FENDER AMPLIFIER

Fender Musical Instruments Corporation, or Fender, is a company that makes musical instruments and equipment. Its **headquarters** is in Los Angeles, California. It is one of the world's top musical instrument companies. Fender also includes the Squier, Gretsch, Jackson, EVH, and Charvel **brands**. In 2020, the company earned more than $700 million in sales!

Fender is best known for its electric guitars, bass guitars, and **amplifiers**. It also makes **acoustic** guitars, ukuleles, mandolins, and banjos. Fender's music **accessories**, such as picks and guitar straps, are also popular. Fender helps musicians sound their best!

FENDER HEADQUARTERS

LOS ANGELES, CALIFORNIA

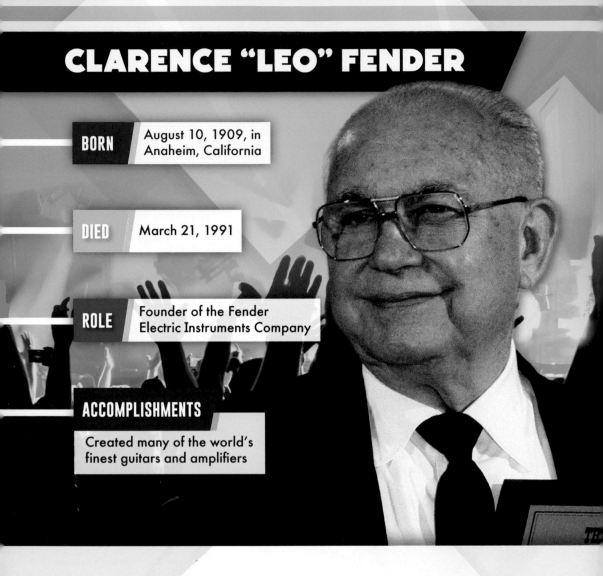

CLARENCE "LEO" FENDER

BORN August 10, 1909, in Anaheim, California

DIED March 21, 1991

ROLE Founder of the Fender Electric Instruments Company

ACCOMPLISHMENTS

Created many of the world's finest guitars and amplifiers

Fender was founded by Leo Fender. He was born in 1909 in Anaheim, California. From a young age, Leo liked to tinker with electronics. A visit to his uncle's auto shop inspired him even more. He saw a radio his uncle had built. Leo wanted to know how it worked. He taught himself how to build and fix radios.

In 1938, Leo started a radio repair business in Fullerton, California. He also built amps and **public address systems**. Musicians began coming to Leo to buy equipment to boost their guitars' sounds.

WOOD AMPS

Leo used wood such as maple and walnut to make his early amps. Today, these amps are known as "woodies."

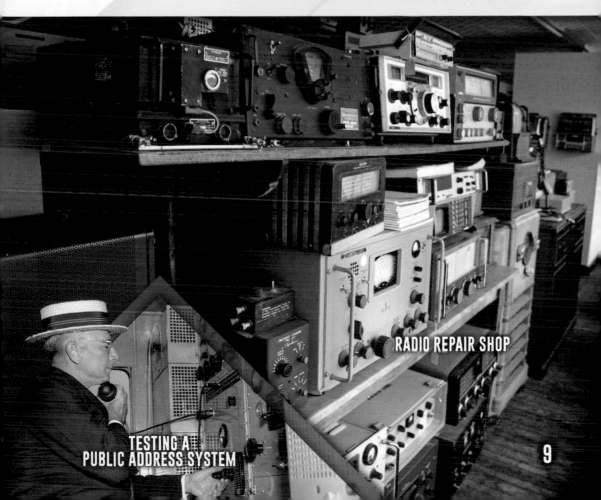

RADIO REPAIR SHOP

TESTING A PUBLIC ADDRESS SYSTEM

In 1943, Leo partnered with Doc Kauffman to start K&F. This company built lap steel guitars. These guitars had an electric **pickup** that Leo invented. Doc left the company in 1946. Leo renamed the business to Fender Electric Instruments Company. His dream was to make high-quality, affordable guitars.

K&F LAP STEEL GUITAR

CUTAWAY

PICKUP

ESQUIRE

GEORGE FULLERTON

Around this time, most guitarists played hollow-bodied guitars through amps. This often created unwanted **feedback**. In the late 1940s, Leo began working with George Fullerton to make the Esquire. This solid-body electric guitar had one **cutaway** and one pickup. It was less likely to have feedback. It came out in 1950.

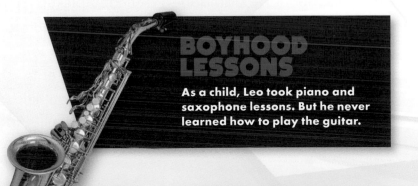

BOYHOOD LESSONS

As a child, Leo took piano and saxophone lessons. But he never learned how to play the guitar.

11

TELECASTER

TRUSS ROD

Leo realized the Esquire could still be improved. He added
a **truss rod** for support. He also added a second pickup for
better sound. It became the Broadcaster. In 1951, Leo changed
the guitar's name to the Telecaster. At first, some people said
it looked like a boat paddle. But its bright sound and great
quality won people over. The Telecaster became a huge hit!

In 1951, the company also released the Precision Bass, or P-Bass. It was the first electric bass that could be played like a guitar. Bass players loved its small size and full sound!

EARLY FENDER GUITARS

1950	ESQUIRE
1950	BROADCASTER/ TELECASTER
1951	PRECISION BASS
1954	STRATOCASTER
1958	JAZZMASTER

Fender continued to grow. In 1954, the company released the Stratocaster, or Strat. It had two cutaways and three single-coil pickups. A new feature called a **tremolo bar** helped players create a more colorful sound. In time, the Strat's design would become standard for electric guitars. It became one of the most recognized guitars on the planet!

In 1958, Fender released the Jazzmaster guitar. It was designed especially for jazz musicians. But to Fender's surprise, other types of musicians began to favor it. It became popular throughout the 1960s.

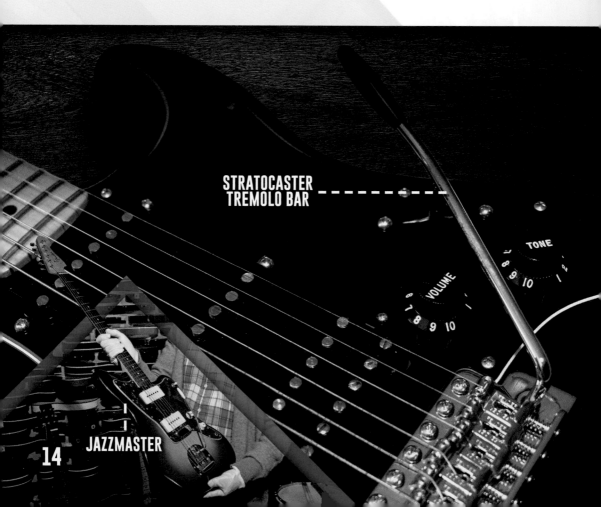

STRATOCASTER
TREMOLO BAR

TONE

VOLUME

JAZZMASTER

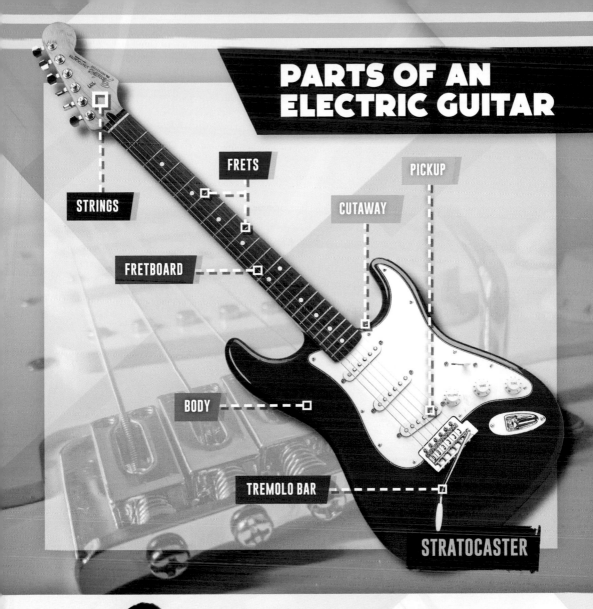

PARTS OF AN ELECTRIC GUITAR

FRETS

STRINGS

PICKUP

CUTAWAY

FRETBOARD

BODY

TREMOLO BAR

STRATOCASTER

A STAR PERFORMANCE

Musician Jimi Hendrix famously played "The Star-Spangled Banner" on his Stratocaster at the 1969 Woodstock Music and Art Fair. The performance put the guitar in the spotlight!

15

CBS HEADQUARTERS
NEW YORK, NEW YORK

1960s FENDER
ADVERTISEMENT

Leo became ill in 1964. He decided to sell the company. In January 1965, CBS bought Fender for $13 million. CBS had no experience in the **industry**. They cut corners to save money. Many people believed the quality of Fender products declined. Over time, sales fell. CBS decided to let Fender go.

In March 1985, CBS sold Fender to a group of Fender employees for $12.5 million. The new owners changed the company's name to Fender Musical Instruments Corporation. Their goal was to build better instruments. They wanted to make Fender an industry leader again.

FENDER TIMELINE

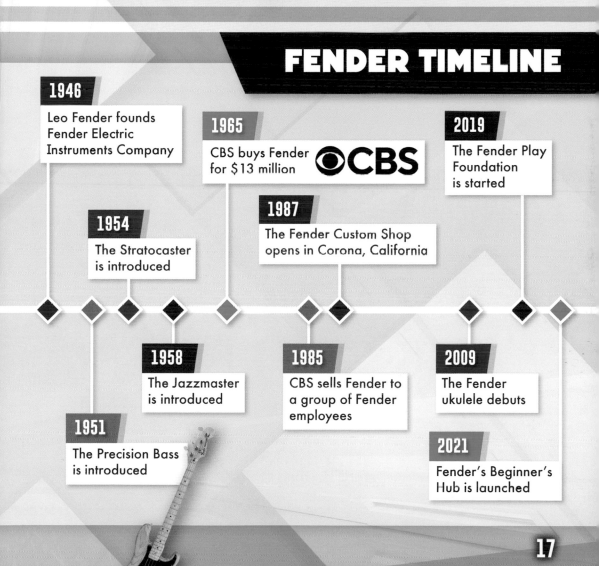

1946
Leo Fender founds Fender Electric Instruments Company

1954
The Stratocaster is introduced

1951
The Precision Bass is introduced

1958
The Jazzmaster is introduced

1965
CBS buys Fender for $13 million
CBS

1987
The Fender Custom Shop opens in Corona, California

1985
CBS sells Fender to a group of Fender employees

2019
The Fender Play Foundation is started

2009
The Fender ukulele debuts

2021
Fender's Beginner's Hub is launched

Fender's new owners faced a problem. CBS did not include any factories in the sale. For a few months, Fender mainly sold products made in Japan. In October 1985, the company opened a factory in Corona, California. Two years later, it opened a factory in Ensenada, Mexico. Fender finally began rebuilding!

The company opened the Fender Custom Shop at the Corona factory in 1987. There, master builders made custom guitars for musicians and collectors. Fender also launched the American Standard Series of guitars. It included the Stratocaster and the Stratocaster Plus. These guitars flew off the shelves!

FENDER FACTORY
CORONA, CALIFORNIA

AMERICAN STANDARD
SERIES GUITAR

TOP SERIES

The Player Series replaced the American Standard Series in 2018. It is one of Fender's top-selling lines!

FENDER AMPS

HOT ROD DELUXE AMP

Fender began to see huge growth. By the late 1990s, the Ensenada factory was making around 150,000 instruments each year. The Corona factory was making around 85,000. Fender amps were also gaining fans. The Hot Rod Deluxe, introduced in 1996, would become one of the world's most popular amps!

Other new products followed. In 2009, the company released its first ukulele. People loved its quality sound and affordable price. The following year, the company released the Acoustasonic Telecaster. This electric guitar was made to produce the sounds of an acoustic guitar.

FENDER
UKELELE

THE MUSIC CONTINUES

FENDER HARMONICA

Fender's success continued in the 2010s. Its headquarters moved to Los Angeles, California, in 2016. The company also increased its presence in Australia with the launch of Fender Music Australia. In 2017, the company released its first harmonicas. The Alternate Reality Series was launched in 2019. It includes several unusual guitars. The Powercaster and the Meteora HH are popular.

During this time, Fender also expanded into teaching. In 2017, the company launched an online program called Fender Play. It offers guitar, bass, and ukulele lessons. Students can choose from more than 1,000 songs to learn!

TOP-SELLING FENDER ELECTRIC GUITARS IN 2022

PLAYER SERIES STRATOCASTER

SQUIER AFFINITY SERIES TELECASTER

PLAYER SERIES TELECASTER

AMERICAN PROFESSIONAL II SERIES TELECASTER

AMERICAN PROFESSIONAL II SERIES STRATOCASTER

In 2021, the company launched an online program called Beginner's Hub. It helps new players choose instruments and learn how to play songs. Fender also bought a music technology company called PreSonus in 2021. It makes equipment and **software** to record and mix music. Fender continues to improve its **digital** amps, too.

AMERICAN VINTAGE II

Fender rolled out the American Vintage II Series in 2022. Its instruments are designed like those built in the 1950s, 1960s, and 1970s.

PRESONUS RECORDING EQUIPMENT

EVH STAR
ELECTRIC GUITAR

JACKSON GUITARS

New releases from other Fender brands also dazzle musicians. EVH debuted its limited edition Star electric guitars in 2023. Jackson unveiled bold new guitars in 2023 for its X Series electric guitars. One has black-and-white checks!

PLAYING IT FORWARD

Fender inspires kids to become musicians. In 2019, it started the Fender Play **Foundation**. This organization gives kids musical instruments and lessons. In its first year, the foundation gave thousands of musical instruments to kids. It gave 2,750 ukeleles and acoustic guitars to students in Hawaii in 2019.

TEAM PLAYER

Billie Eilish is part of the Fender Play Foundation team. She gives ukuleles and music lessons to kids in her hometown of Highland Park, California!

In 2020, the foundation teamed up with Los Angeles schools. Students receive an acoustic, electric, or bass guitar, or a ukulele. They also get free music lessons! Today, more than 24,000 students and 70 teachers participate in the program. Fender's goal is to reach one million students by the year 2030!

GIVING BACK

750 ACOUSTIC GUITARS
GIVEN TO STUDENTS IN HAWAII IN 2019

2,000 UKULELES
GIVEN TO STUDENTS IN HAWAII IN 2019

OVER $1 MILLION
GIVEN BY THE FENDER PLAY FOUNDATION SINCE 2019

JAMMING WITH FENDER

NATIONAL ASSOCIATION OF MUSIC MERCHANTS SHOW
ANAHEIM, CALIFORNIA

Fender fans can enjoy the brand in many ways. The National Association of Music Merchants (NAMM) Show features around 7,000 music brands, including Fender. They share their new products in booths and on stage. Fans can learn about new guitars and other products.

In 2019, Fender started the Fender Next program. Fender selects 25 talented guitarists from around the world to partner with the company. The program provides the players with gear and helps promote their music. Fender hits the right note with musicians everywhere!

MOD SHOP

Musicians can use Fender's Mod Shop to create their own guitars. They can choose their own colors and add-ons. A team of builders makes the instruments by hand!

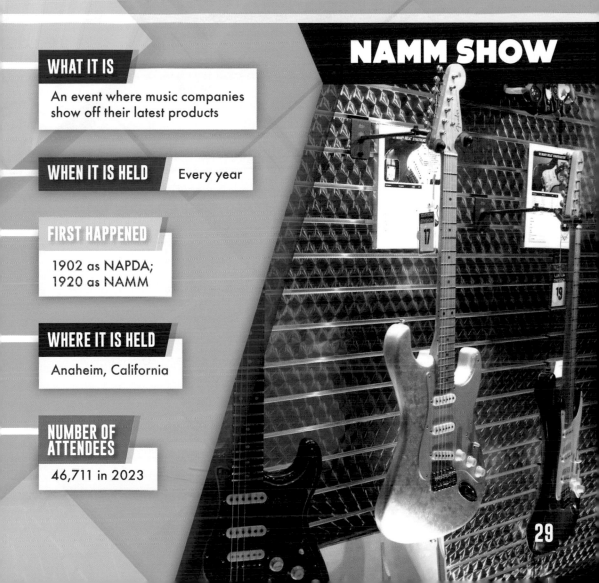

NAMM SHOW

WHAT IT IS

An event where music companies show off their latest products

WHEN IT IS HELD Every year

FIRST HAPPENED

1902 as NAPDA;
1920 as NAMM

WHERE IT IS HELD

Anaheim, California

NUMBER OF ATTENDEES

46,711 in 2023

GLOSSARY

accessories—items added to something else to make it more useful or attractive

acoustic—related to guitars with hollow bodies that use strings to make sound

amplifiers—devices that increase the volume of musical instruments; amplifiers are often called amps.

brands—categories of products all made by the same company

cutaway—an indentation in the upper part of a guitar next to the neck

digital—related to electronic or computer technology

feedback—a screeching sound caused by sound moving from a guitar to an amp and back again

foundation—an organization that gives money to people or groups in need

fretboard—a piece of wood that sticks out from the body of a guitar; the fretboard is the front of the guitar's neck.

headquarters—a company's main office

industry—businesses that provide a certain product or service

pickup—a device that changes the vibration of guitar strings into electrical signals

public address systems—electronic systems with microphones, amps, and speakers that are used in public areas

software—computer programs that do specific tasks

tremolo bar—a lever attached to a guitar; a player presses the tremolo bar to raise or lower pitch.

truss rod—a thin metal shaft that runs the length of a guitar's neck to give it support

TO LEARN MORE

AT THE LIBRARY

Hoena, Blake. *The Electric Guitar: A Graphic History*. Minneapolis, Minn.: Graphic Universe, 2021.

Mahin, Michael. *Gizmos, Gadgets, and Guitars: The Story of Leo Fender*. New York, N.Y.: Henry Holt and Company, 2021.

Morland, Charlie. *Music and How it Works: The Complete Guide for Kids*. New York, N.Y.: DK Publishing, 2020.

ON THE WEB

FACTSURFER

Factsurfer.com gives you a safe, fun way to find more information.

1. Go to www.factsurfer.com.

2. Enter "Fender" into the search box and click 🔍.

3. Select your book cover to see a list of related content.

INDEX